DERMATOLOGY
for kids

Copyright © 2022 Betty Nguyen & Brandon Pham

All rights reserved. No part of this book may be reproduced or used in any manner without the prior written permission of the copyright owner, except for the use of brief quotations in a book review.

First paperback edition March 2022

Book design by Betty Nguyen & Brandon Pham

ISBN 978-1-957557-00-7 (paperback)

Printed in the United States of America

Published by Black Phoenix Press

www.mdforkids.org

Disclaimer: Contents of this book are for informational purposes only. No material in this book is intended to provide, or be a substitute for, professional medical advice.

To the friends and family who have supported and loved us unconditionally, and to the mentors who have guided and taught us more that we could have imagined:

Thank you.

Betty & Brandon

Dermatology
(dur-muh-TAA-luh-jee)

the branch of medicine concerned with the study and treatment of disorders and diseases of the skin

Our entire body is covered in **skin**.

Skin protects us when we fall down.

Skin protects us from getting too cold or too hot.

Skin protects us from germs that can make us sick.

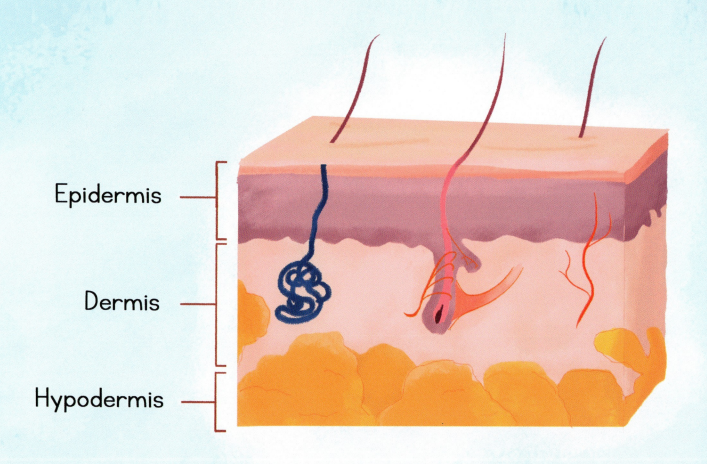

The skin is made up of 3 layers.

The *outer* layer of skin is called the **epidermis.**

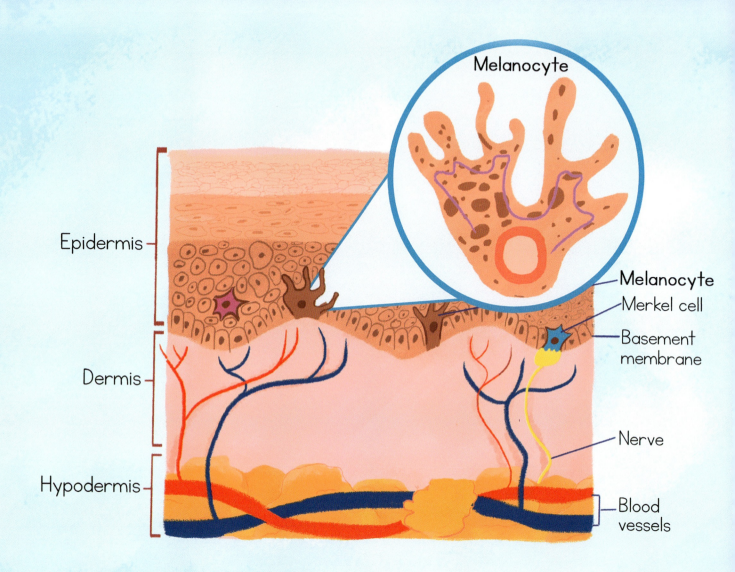

Melanocytes live in the epidermis.
Melanocytes make **melanin**,
a pigment that gives our skin color.

People with *more* melanin have *darker* skin.
People with *less* melanin have *lighter* skin.

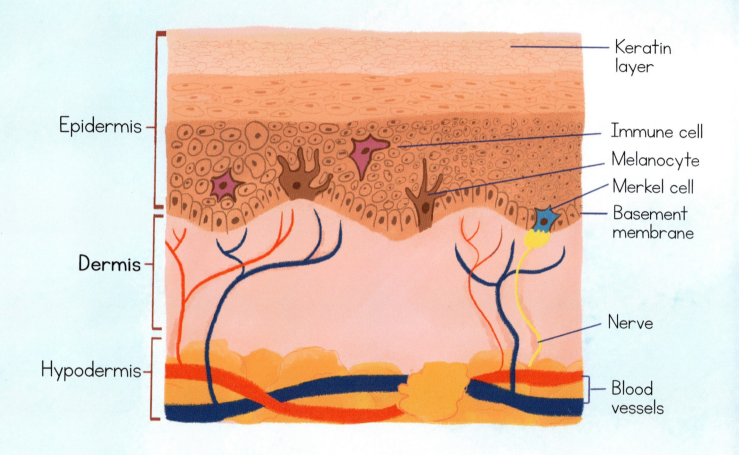

The *middle* layer of skin is called the **dermis.**

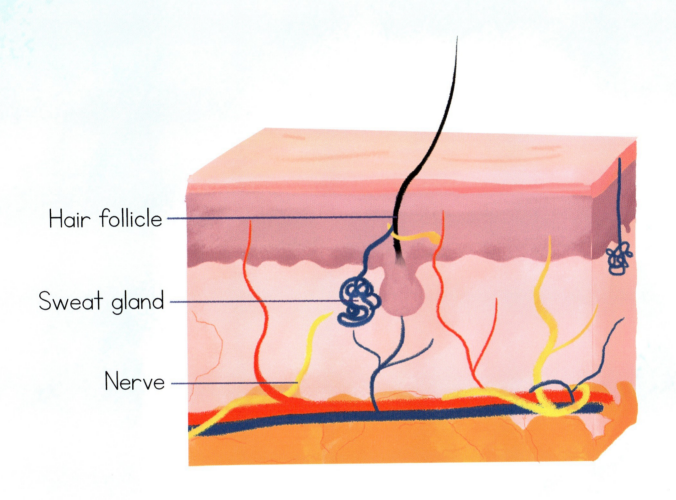

Hair follicles, sweat glands, and nerves live in the dermis.

Hair follicles make hair, which protects our skin and keeps our bodies warm.

Sweat glands make sweat, which keeps our bodies cool.

Nerves help us sense touch, temperature, and pain.

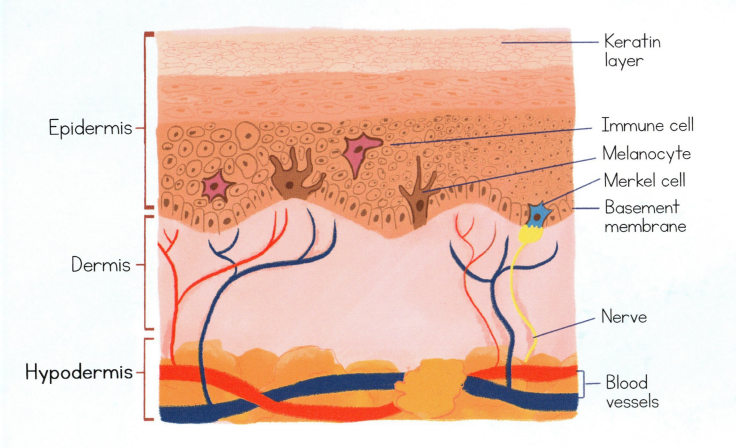

The *inner* layer of skin is called the **hypodermis**.

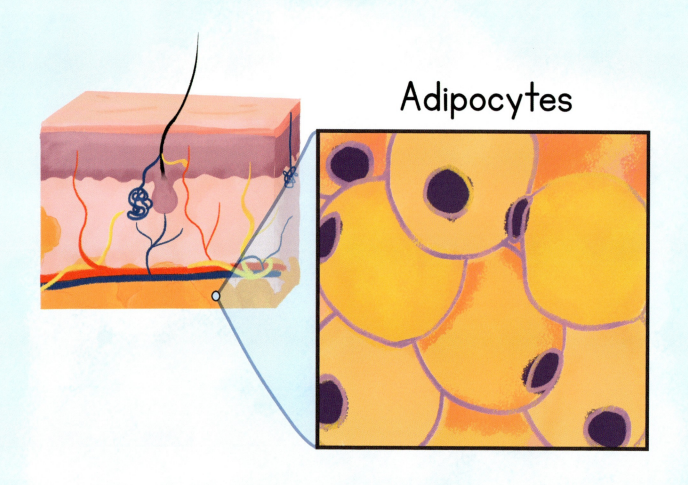

Adipocytes

Adipocytes live in the hypodermis. Adipocytes store fat, which keeps us warm and can be used to make energy.

Our skin also has other important jobs. When we go outside, our skin absorbs energy from sunlight to make **vitamin D**.

With too much sunlight though, our skin can burn.

The good news is that our skin can repair itself. Our body makes a new layer of skin every month!

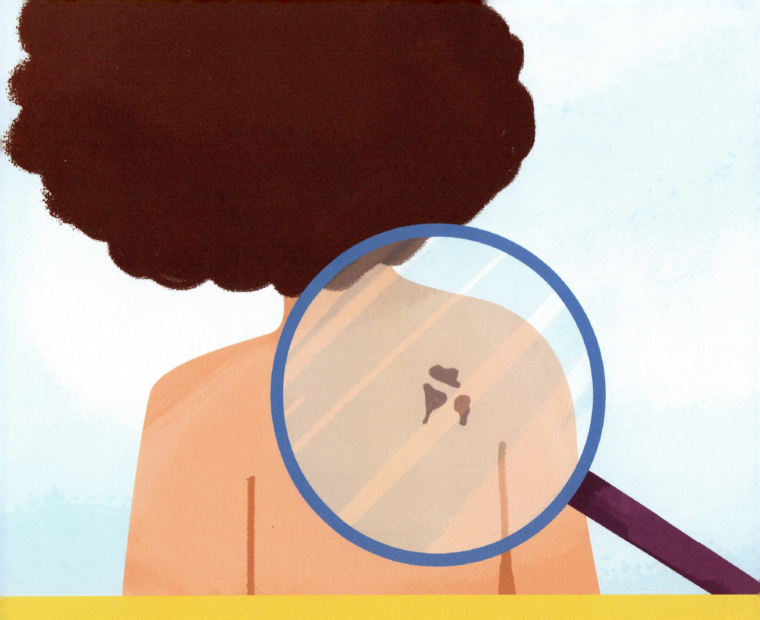

The sun can also cause **melanoma**, a type of skin cancer caused by melanocytes that grow and divide uncontrollably.

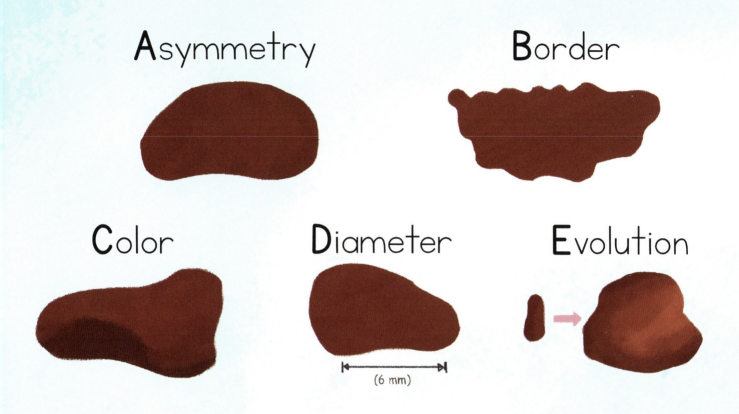

A **mole** is a dark spot on your skin. Most moles are not harmful, but some can be melanoma. You can check your moles for the **ABCDEs** of melanoma.

Melanoma

Normal mole

A is for **asymmetry**.

Melanoma can be asymmetric. That means one half looks different from the other. Normal moles are usually symmetric.

Melanoma

Normal mole

B is for **border**.
Melanoma can have jagged or uneven borders. Normal moles have even and regular borders.

Melanoma   Normal mole

C is for **color**.

Moles with many colors can be melanoma.

Normal moles are usually brown.

Melanoma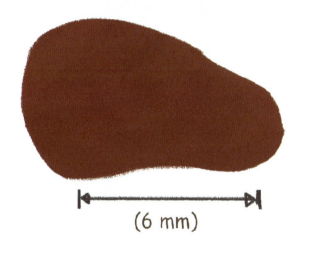

(6 mm)

Normal mole

D is for **diameter**.
Any mole 6 millimeters or bigger can be melanoma. This is about the size of a pencil eraser.

Melanoma
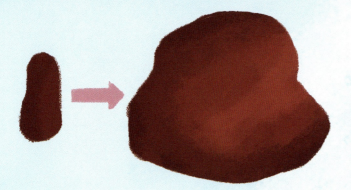

Normal mole

E is for **evolution**.
A mole that gets bigger, changes colors, changes shapes, or starts itching or bleeding can be melanoma.

Wearing a hat and sunscreen protects the skin on your face and body from sunburns and skin cancer.

Skin can have many different colors. No matter the color, we all need skin to keep us safe.

Every day, dermatologists help patients with skin disorders to look, feel, and get better.

Glossary

Adipocyte (uh-DI-puh-site): a cell in the hypodermis that stores fat

Dermis (DUR-mihs): middle layer of the skin

Epidermis (eh-pih-DUR-mihs): outer layer of the skin

Hair follicle: structure in the dermis through which hair grows

Hypodermis (hai-po-DUR-mihs): inner layer of the skin

Melanin (MEH-luh-nin): pigment that gives our skin color

Melanocyte (meh-LAH-no-site): a cell in the epidermis that makes melanin

Melanoma (meh-lah-NO-ma): type of skin cancer caused by melanocytes that grow and divide uncontrollably

Nerve: structure in the dermis that helps us sense touch, temperature, and pain

Sweat gland: structure in the dermis that makes sweat

Vitamin D: a vitamin our body makes when our skin is exposed to sunlight

Let's review what you learned!

1. What is the outer layer of skin called?
2. Melanocytes are found in what layer of the skin?
3. What is the name of the pigment that gives our skin color?
4. What is the middle layer of skin called?
5. Hair follicles are found in what layer of the skin?
6. Sweat glands are found in what layer of the skin?
7. Nerves are found in what layer of the skin?
8. What is the inner layer of skin called?
9. Adipocytes are found in what layer of the skin?
10. Our skin absorbs energy from sunlight to make what vitamin?
11. What is the name of a type of skin cancer caused by melanocytes that grow and divide uncontrollably?
12. What are the ABCDEs of melanoma?
13. What are 2 ways you can protect your skin from the sun?

Your Answers

1. _____
2. _____
3. _____
4. _____
5. _____
6. _____
7. _____
8. _____
9. _____
10. _____
11. _____
12. _____
13. _____

Answer Key

1. Epidermis
2. Epidermis
3. Melanin
4. Dermis
5. Dermis
6. Dermis
7. Dermis
8. Hypodermis
9. Hypodermis
10. Vitamin D
11. Melanoma
12. Asymmetry, Border, Color, Diameter, Evolution
13. Wearing a hat and sunscreen

About the Authors

Betty Nguyen

Betty Nguyen was born in California but spent much of her childhood in Georgia, where her parents worked on a chicken farm. She received a bachelor's degree in Biology from UCLA, where she received a full-ride Gates Millennium Scholarship through the Bill & Melinda Gates Foundation. Betty also received a full-tuition scholarship to attend medical school at the University of California, Riverside. Outside of work, Betty is a certified yoga instructor and licensed scuba diver. She also enjoys journalistic writing, cycling, and walking her two dogs in her free time.

Brandon Pham

Brandon Pham was born and raised in California. He received a bachelor's degree in Microbiology, Immunology, and Molecular Genetics from UCLA, where he was a national Goldwater Scholar. He graduated from Stanford Medical School and is currently completing his residency in ophthalmology at the Bascom Palmer Eye Institute in Miami, Florida. Brandon spent many years teaching for several national test-preparation companies and is passionate about medical education for students of all ages. In his free time, Brandon enjoys traveling, playing tennis, and distance running.

Check out the rest of the books in our series!

www.mdforkids.org

Printed by Amazon Italia Logistica S.r.l.
Torrazza Piemonte (TO), Italy